Stay Balanced While You Study

TRIGGER™
The mental health & wellbeing publisher

Stay Balanced While You Study

BY DR DOMINIQUE THOMPSON

Dr Dominique Thompson is a GP, young people's mental health expert, TEDx speaker, author and educator, with over twenty years of clinical experience caring for students, most recently as director of service at the University of Bristol Students' Health Service. It was for this work that she was named Bristol Healthcare Professional of the Year 2017.

She is a clinical advisor for the Royal College of GPs, and for Student Minds, the UK's student mental health charity. She was the GP member of the NICE Eating Disorders' guidelines development group, and the Universities UK StepChange and Minding Our Future committees. Dominique is also a member of the UK Mental Wellbeing in Higher Education group (MWBHE).

Dominique has helped design apps and websites to support student mental health, and writes books on the topic. She has been interviewed widely, including by the *Guardian* and Radio 4's *Today* programme.

Her TEDx talk entitled 'What I learnt from 78,000 GP consultations with university students' highlights some of the causes behind the recent rise in young people's mental health distress, and suggests ways in which *everyone* can better support the younger generation.

Dominique has now launched her own student health and wellbeing consultancy, Buzz Consulting, to assist organisations in improving their student support offer.

You can follow her on Twitter and on Instagram @drdomthompson.

Stay Balanced While You Study

Make the Most of your Student Experience

DR DOMINIQUE THOMPSON

TRIGGER™
The mental health & wellbeing publisher

First published in Great Britain 2020 by Trigger

Trigger is a trading style of Shaw Callaghan Ltd
& Shaw Callaghan 23 USA, INC.
The Foundation Centre
Navigation House, 48 Millgate, Newark
Nottinghamshire NG24 4TS UK

www.triggerpublishing.com

Text Copyright © 2020 Dr Dominique Thompson

British Library Cataloguing in Publication Data
A CIP catalogue record for this book is available upon request
from the British Library.

ISBN: 9781789561906

This book is also available in the following e-Book formats:

ePUB: 9781789561913

Cover design by stevewilliamscreative.com
Cover illustration: macrovector_official / Freepik

Typeset by Fusion Graphic Design Ltd

Printed and bound in Great Britain by Clays Ltd, Elcograf S.p.A

Paper from responsible sources

For Miguel – You never gave up
– keep going, keep smiling!

Also available in this series:

ROLE DEFINITIONS

A Who's Who of Student Support

Doctor (general practitioner)
A medically qualified doctor who sees people in the community, not in a hospital, and is able to help with all conditions, although they may have a special interest, for example in skin problems or mental health. They are sometimes called a "family doctor", and will often refer to specialists, such as psychiatrists or psychologists, for specific problems.

Counselor
A counselor offers a safe, confidential space for individuals to talk. Counselors help their clients explore their thoughts, feelings and actions to help them come to terms with life and find more hopeful and useful ways to approach their future. Counselors will work in different ways, depending on their training, but will always allow their client to take the lead in what they want to talk about. They do not offer advice, but through the empathic attention they give to their client's words, the client often discovers their own wisdom, helping them to lead a more fulfilling life.

Clinical Psychologist
A person who specializes in psychological or emotional conditions, and mental health disorders. They will have specialized in the study of clinical psychology and will usually

have a doctorate or PhD (though they're not medically qualified, and will not able to prescribe medication). They assess people and diagnose mental health conditions or problems. They are trained in using talking and behavioral interventions specifically tailored to treat psychological disorders. They may use a range of therapy approaches, which vary from psychodynamic to cognitive behavioral therapy, family and couples' therapies to interpersonal approaches. They base their assessment and treatment methods on scientific principles and outcomes and will use the best evidenced method that helps to treat an individual.

Therapist
A term for professionals who use talking and behavioral therapies to support people with mental health conditions.

Psychiatrist
A medically qualified doctor who specializes in mental health conditions – also called psychiatric conditions – who can assess, make a diagnosis, offer advice, and prescribe medications. A psychiatrist is the only person who can prescribe specialist medications. They work with GPs, therapists, psychologists and counselors and will usually recommend a type of talking or behavioral treatment.

CONTENTS

INTRODUCTION

What Is This Book About?

This is a book about balance, and finding *your* balance. Not the sort of balance that may involve sitting cross-legged whilst humming, though that can be very relaxing. *This* is the kind of balance that will enable you to feel calm in the face of life's challenges.

When humans get stressed, we tend to find the best way of coping *in that moment*. But not all of those methods will be healthy. We "get through" and survive, but at what cost to ourselves and our wellbeing?

Take a moment to think about what *you* do when you're stressed? What is your go-to coping strategy? Food, alcohol, buying yourself a treat, getting high, or even going so far as to hurt yourself physically, for example by cutting your skin? Sometimes these actions can help temporarily, but in the long term they are not ideal.

When stressed or in need of distraction from emotional pain, students, like anyone else, sometimes drink too much alcohol, use drugs, eat too much (or too little), take unhealthy risks, gamble or even physically hurt themselves. These are the most common coping strategies for students and young people in particular, and in many ways these methods do actually help, taking your mind off the immediate stress. But maybe there are other (better) ways to cope. Ways that will help you to do better in life, study more effectively, achieve more, have stronger friendships and relationships and get more out of life, without the risks associated with alcohol, drugs, gambling or other risky behaviors.

On the other hand, when life is going well, it is completely normal and psychologically beneficial to want to mark our achievements, often with the use of food, alcohol or drugs as *rewards*. So, as well as their use as coping methods, we will also consider how these strategies, when employed to congratulate ourselves, might be worth reviewing and challenging, as there might be healthier ways to applaud our achievements when we pass an exam, land a job or promotion, or win a match. Perhaps there is a way to mark these events in ways that are not "potentially harmful."

This little book is not the fun police!

No one is trying to stop you from occasionally clicking "buy now" on those gold high-heeled boots when you're in need of cheering up or from drunk messaging your secret crush at 3 a.m. (these things happen!). It's fine to have a couple of drinks with friends after a long week, or an occasional slice of cake. But the words a couple or occasional are key here.

There is nothing stopping you from being spontaneous or having fun. But this book is here to help anyone who thinks that their actions sometimes feel out of control, who believes that their daily choices might not be that healthy or helpful and to help anyone who is struggling with behaviors that might even be self-harmful or self-destructive.

Lots of people have habits in life that help them to cope that they wish they could better control or even stop. They may recognize that their own reactions to stress are less than ideal, or other people may have commented on or criticized these habits and behaviors.

Often even if they wanted to stop or cut back on those behaviors that might be harming them, they feel that they can't always help themselves.

How might this book help?

The chapters will describe:

- some common behaviors that can lead students to feel out of control.
- times when you might be more at risk of taking things too far.
- what to watch out for in yourself or in friends,
- and how you can help yourself (or others) to feel calm and find balance.
- where more help is available and who to turn to if you need more specialist advice.

With this information, you may start to realize that you have been drifting into bad habits or stuck in an unhelpful rut for a while. The hope is that you will recognize any unhealthy or unhelpful coping strategies you may be using and consider changes to your behavior, in turn finding better ways to manage your stress (and "reward" habits).

However, this book:

- is not about blame; it is written with compassion.
- will try to help you find a better balance in your life, while still having fun.
- is clear that difficult things happen to all of us in life, so finding positive, sustainable ways to cope is vital.

If you want to stay balanced in difficult times, this book is written for you.

Who might need extra support to avoid unhelpful or potentially self-harmful behaviors?

Some people lead difficult and complicated lives. Others less so, but we *all* suffer tough times. You may be dealing wit difficult life events, past trauma or traumatic incidents, crise or bereavement. If you are in this situation, it is likely tha you will seek ways to cope. Some of these will be healthy for example, through counseling, exercise and lots of rest. Whereas other choices might be unhealthy, but may still *seem* to help. Initially, you may feel like you have the choices and subsequent behaviors under control, but that control can start to slide slowly, or even fall away suddenly without warning. You may find yourself binge eating, binge drinking, using more drugs or even cutting your skin. Before you realize it, you're no longer in charge of your own actions.

Some students may find the stressful situations in life *extra* distressing because they have to deal with prejudice, discrimination or hate. For example, students who are of certain ethnicities, religions or LGBTQ+. They may also look for ways to cope with this additional pressure, again, through restricting food, using recreational drugs or by self-harming to numb or distract from their suffering and anxiety.

Students with caring responsibilities (carers), those with family friction at home, or those who are estranged from their families can also find life especially demanding and messy, and for them too, it may feel natural to seek comfort and relief in potentially unhealthy ways.

Any one of us can struggle at times, and although those from particular backgrounds (such as students leaving the care system) may have specific hurdles to overcome, students come from such a wide variety of cultures and circumstances (international, mature, first in a family to attend university, commuter, etc.) that you can see how *any* student might struggle to always stay emotionally well, and might occasionally (or frequently) use coping behaviors that are, in fact, harmful.

CHAPTER 1

COPING STRATEGIES – THE GOOD, THE BAD AND THE UGLY

People do many things to cope with emotional or physical pain they might be suffering – too many to write about in one (little) book – so we will focus on six specific topics. The principles and advice, however, will be applicable to many more scenarios and challenging situations, so hopefully it will be helpful for you, whatever your unique circumstances. The topics we will cover are:

- Risk-taking behaviours
- Alcohol
- Drugs
- Gambling/gaming
- Food
- Physical self-harm

Having discussed each of these common coping strategies a little more, we will suggest ways to reduce their potential harm as well as looking at healthier alternatives to try. Each chapter will include real, anonymized stories from students who have been in the same boat as you and have struggled when life threw them a curveball. At the end, there is a list of specialist resources in case you decide to seek further advice.

Do I Need Help?

Signs that you (or someone else) might be struggling.

There are a few warning flags that you can watch out for if you think you (or your friend) might be finding it hard to cope with life.

Your behavior may become erratic, you might stop following your usual routines, your sleep pattern can be disrupted, and your mood may be all over the place. Your weight can climb slowly or drop away, or your skin and hair might deteriorate. You might stop doing some of the things you should be doing, like turning up for lectures or work, and you might even stop doing the things you really like doing to relax or have fun, like seeing friends, sports or other favorite activities.

It can be common to cover things up and not let anyone know (even those you trust) what's happening to you, which can add significant stress at an already difficult time.

In certain situations, such as with gambling or substance and alcohol misuse, the most obvious initial negative effect can be on your wallet, and it may be this that first alerts you to consider how much you are spending on coping with distress.

However, you don't always need to reach a point where your struggle affects your relationships, work, finance, or studies for your coping strategies to be unbalanced. Rather, it may be that you manage to keep coping by using behaviors that are paradoxically both helpful *and* self-harmful. It may be that you can only relax because you're drunk or using pills, or that the reason you will be able to function tomorrow is because you cut or hurt yourself today. It may not be healthy, but it's getting you through. You are "coping", although such approaches could lead to a damaging negative cycle of behaviors.

It's complicated.

Sometimes we don't realize that things are becoming harder to manage until someone else notices. It may only be when a friend or family member comments on your unreliability or your mood swings or changes in your normal habits that you take a moment to reflect on what might be going on, how you are getting through each day, and whether or not it might be time to make some healthier choices and changes in your life.

It may only be when you are failing academically, your partner leaves you, you fall out with your friends, or you reach rock bottom that you feel able to make any changes, but hopefully you will be aware of the need for better strategies much sooner than that. We are all human, and none of us have all the answers in life, so asking for help from others, reading about what useful approaches you might try, and talking about your struggles is a good way to start.

Where to Go for Help

Remember that in every college or university there are teams of staff ready and waiting just to help students who are struggling, whose entire role is student support: counselors, disability advisors, wellbeing advisors, doctors, chaplains, therapists and psychologists. The academic teams (tutors, lecturers, professors and admin staff) are also trained to help students who reach out and may need signposting to the specialist student support teams.

You are not alone, and if you are not sure where to start, then first speak to a member of staff you trust. Whether that is the librarian, the security guard, the receptionist who says hello every morning, or the accommodation team member you know best, they are all there to help you.

Fun versus Risk

It is important to remember that lots of people use alcohol or take risks for fun; it doesn't have to be self-harmful. This book focuses on helping those people for whom these behaviors are becoming, or have become a *problem*, and who want to minimize the risk of making their life more complicated than it already is.

If you like a few drinks with friends, enjoy dessert occasionally or choose to drive fast or go mountain boarding at weekends but feel happy with your choices and enjoy the buzz, then you may not need this book. Having fun and taking good, considered risks is all part of being human!

But if you frequently turn to weed, pills or powder and booze to get through social occasions, often eat to make yourself feel better, starve yourself to take back "control", gamble regularly for the adrenaline rush, or have sex with strangers to feel a thrill (or loved) despite the risks, then this book may help by sharing some insights and by giving you an opportunity to step back and think differently about your long-term choices and options.

Avoiding Unhealthy "Rewards"

If you use cake, alcohol or drugs as a default to reward ("treat") yourself for getting through exams, finishing an essay, landing a place in a sports team, doing well in anything, etc., then you may also wish to consider awarding yourself healthier and less potentially harmful prizes for winning at life.

If you need inspiration for treats and rewards (because you're worth it!) instead of cake/alcohol/drugs/gaming/gambling, then read on.

Top tip for rewarding yourself

It may help to consider each of *your five senses* and see what might *heighten* those in a positive way as a reward and distance you from any negative feelings or emotions – if that is why you are treating yourself to something nice.

Think about what might lift you or help you to feel better, and allow yourself to feel indulged or special when you need to feel like giving yourself a pat on the back (or soothed). Think of something that you will enjoy reading, tasting, feeling, sensing or listening to, as a guide to what will work for you, with examples suggested below.

Treat yourself to any of these occasionally – or think of your own special treats!

- New toiletries (e.g. hair conditioner, perfume, lipstick, face cream).
- A ticket to the movies or a stage show.
- Download some music or an audiobook.
- Buy a subscription to your favorite magazine or curl up with a book.
- Binge watch that TV show you love or that everyone has been talking about.
- Try on or buy some new or preloved shoes.
- If you're into a specific sport, such as cycling or running, then get yourself a small accessory or new piece of kit.
- Buy or make some nice "proper" coffee.
- Make a photo album from all your photos.
- Book a massage or even a spa day – look for special offers or check discount websites for great deals.
- Go and watch a sporting event.
- Book a session with a personal trainer. (Many universities offer this for free!).
- Decorate your room.
- Buy yourself a pot plant or flowers to bring the outside in.

There are many ways to make yourself feel great and reward yourself when life goes well, so try to get into the habit of using ways that don't have the potential to be harmful as a side effect (like alcohol).

There is a coping strategy for every situation (although sometimes we also need help from other people to get through), so make your choice of coping mechanism carefully, from the good, the bad and the ugly.

CHAPTER 2

RISKY BEHAVIORS

Why do People Take Risks?

We do it for fun, for a buzz or thrill, for distraction, or to feel more alive. To bond with others and feel part of a crowd, or to feel less alone. Our brains are wired to reward us when we take risks, to "light up" when we do exciting things and then to cause an adrenaline rush in our bodies as we experience the flush of pleasure.[i] Taking risks is part of who we are as humans, and never more so than in teenagers and young adults, in whom the brain reacts most powerfully to potential danger or excitement. In short, risks makes us feel good.

However, although our biology may push us to do thrilling or hazardous things, we must consciously decide how far we should go. It is important to remember that **all actions have consequences**. *Positive* actions, such as volunteering, usually have a *positive* impact on us, whilst *negative* or highly risky actions may appear to have positive outcomes in the short term, but are more likely to have *negative* consequences later on in our lives. Take time to weigh up the choices you make.

Why do we do things we know may not be good for us, and may even be self-destructive?

How might this play out in your life? You might pursue dangerous sports, smoke, drive too fast, or you might choose to engage in unprotected sex, or go home with a stranger after a party. Putting yourself in jeopardy can sometimes be unintentional, a consequence of seeking out fun, thrills and distraction. Sometimes it is less an "active choice" and more the result of a complex situation where you find yourself vulnerable and at risk of being hurt by others or by the activity, such as getting drunk alone or taking drugs with people you don't know well.

It may even be that you don't care what happens to you, or you feel too depressed or numb to protect yourself. It's not your fault, of course, but such situations are highly risky and can lead to difficult and even traumatic consequences.

> **Remember:** Support workers and staff are very familiar with the difficult scenarios in which students and young people can find themselves, and are keen to support you, and help in a non-judgemental manner if you need it.

Risk-taking behaviors can also, in the worst cases, lead to death, through accidents (for example, from careless driving, incidents whilst traveling, or falls from a height). Accidental death is the second most common cause of death in young adults after suicide.[ii] Risk-taking may be a normal behavior for many young people, but if you can balance the thrill of doing something *exciting* with the potential *danger* it might put you in, and come down on the right side of that equation, it could literally save your life! That equation is all about calculating risk (while still having fun!).

Every time you make a decision about wearing a seatbelt or a bike helmet, using a condom, having "one last drink", smoking a cigarette or sending a text whilst driving you are taking a risk, with your health, with your safety (and others') and sometimes with the law. You are calculating the pros and cons of taking that risk, and (even if only for a very brief moment) you are weighing up your options. And depending on what else is happening for you in your life, – your relationships, your studies or in your emotions right at that moment – your decision to take the chance (or not) will be affected.

Context matters, so knowing that lots of factors, such as your mood or other people, will affect your decision-making may be enough to help you stop and think a little longer.

So don't rush in. Take a moment to "do the maths" and calculate your risk!

When Mental Health Plays a Role

Certain conditions such as bipolar disorder (which is a mental health condition that leads to severe highs and lows of mood, as well as sleep and energy changes) can also lead to episodes where taking risks becomes more likely. This is often as part of feeling "hypomanic" or "manic", which involves losing *insight* (the ability to understand the reality of a situation), and feeling very elated ("up") in mood. During such states, the person's sense of danger, and ability to judge a situation, may be reduced, and may lead them to behave in ways that would not be usual for them when they are well. They may even be shocked by their own behaviour when their mood and insight return to normal.

Bipolar disorder is not the only mental health condition which can lead to risky behavior, of course, so no assumptions should be made if you notice this behavior in yourself or friends. However, it is a good example of where mental health plays a key role in changing behavior, and where professional help will be needed. Other conditions associated with higher risk-taking include substance misuse, attention deficit hyperactivity disorder, emotional instability and psychosis. However, risky behavior can be a normal part of life, so if you're not sure what to do or what is happening, share your concerns with someone you trust and make a plan about what to do next.

Mia's Story

Mia's three flatmates first noticed changes in her behavior about halfway through the term when they heard her moving around the flat at night, singing and seemingly very happy, but they had not thought much of it. She seemed very "up" and chatty, maybe even talking a little too fast, but they weren't really worried. She mentioned that she was planning to go out and party more, and would tell them after how she had been dancing all night, and what an amazing time she had had. But she got irritable if her flatmates tried to suggest that she get some rest, sleep or eat a bit more. They were starting to worry, but unsure how to help.

The first night she brought home a man at 3 a.m., the flatmates were understanding and the second night, tolerant. But by the third night of meeting another strange man in their bathroom, the other girls were feeling stressed. Mia seemed to be taking risks, not just with her own health and wellbeing (by having sex with men she didn't know), but potentially with their safety too by inviting several different strangers into their home. And she didn't seem to realize ... or care.

They decided to speak to her about it sensitively, but she became upset, so they asked her if they could call her mum for advice and help. One of the girls also decided to speak to a university counselor to seek professional support about what their next steps might be. They were right to do so, because Mia (without anyone realizing) was developing a "manic episode" (bipolar disorder) for the first time in her life: a rare but serious event that needed professional intervention.

Healthy Ways to Manage or Reduce Negative Risky Behavior

If you want to take steps to change your behavior, to still have fun but protect yourself more or stay safe, then there are lots of practical things you can do to help you reflect, and then slowly make changes in your life. Some of the suggestions below will also focus on how you can still get a thrill without exposing yourself to unnecessary danger.

Build confidence and self-esteem

Ask yourself, 'What am I good at?' and focus on that. Spend time building on your best qualities. Are you great with people, a fantastic artist, a problem-solver? Develop your skills. This will help to build your confidence and self-esteem and make you more able to avoid negative behaviors when you feel down. Find good role models in people you admire, who live in a way you would enjoy but also feel safe with.

Be aware of the impact on friends and family

Take time to sit and think about how your behavior may be affecting those you care about. This can be a powerful way to motivate yourself to change things, and you might like to write down five things that will be *better* when you make some positive changes.

Write yourself motivational Post-it notes

Or make a note on your phone about 'What would different look like?' Think about what your aims and goals are in trying to make changes. You might hope to wake up feeling clear-headed every day or feel fitter. You might like to save some money for a vacation or a day out with friends.

Ask yourself what would it look like if the positive changes you make actually happened? Visualize that scenario, then think about what you need to do to get you there, and keep going, even if it doesn't go right first time, or you feel like sometimes you fail – don't give up! Write it down and keep reminding yourself. Avoid blame and feeling guilty if it all goes wrong – simply try again.

Avoid alcohol or drugs if you're feeling vulnerable

Drinking and taking drugs are likely to make you more exposed and susceptible to taking risks because your ability to calculate danger and weigh up the pros and cons of your decision will be numbed and clouded. If you are already in a situation that puts you at potential risk, like out with people you don't know well, then avoid adding alcohol or drugs to the mix and making yourself unsafe.[iii] It is also important to be aware that you are more likely to take risks when with your peers, so bear this in mind when you feel influenced to drink more or drive faster, for example. If you are feeling low or anxious, this can make you more likely to take risks, and less able to be objective, too.

Develop positive risk outlets[iv]

There are many ways to get a kick out of life without putting yourself in danger, so here are a few suggestions of ways to take positive, "good" risks. Sport is an obvious one, but maybe try something you haven't done before or something silly like go-karting, and take the risk that you will be rubbish at first, but think of the thrill as you get better! Get outside and into nature – hiking, climbing, kayaking, surfing all involve dealing with the unknown and the elements, but are great for an adrenaline rush, and for the CV.[v] Get into performing arts; doing live stage shows really focuses the mind and gives a huge endorphin ("happy hormone") rush too. Volunteer in an unfamiliar charity or group, meet new people, stretch your boundaries, or travel overseas and test your limits, but take *good* risks.

Supporting a Friend Who is Taking Risks

It can be hard to know where to start if a friend is behaving in a way that worries you. You want to be supportive, but not a "killjoy" or "boring" in their eyes. You want to do the best thing for *them*, but not be seen as judging their life choices, or interfering. It's a tricky balance to achieve, and an "intervention" may not be appreciated. Ultimately you will have to do what feels right to you and what you are comfortable with because you have to be able to live with your decisions and actions in the longer term, but here are some suggestions about how to approach a complex or delicate situation.

- **Pick your moment carefully.** Don't try to have a difficult conversation when your friend is not in a good place to listen or speak calmly with you. Find a time when you are both relaxed and are unlikely to be disturbed or interrupted. Allow time to talk but also be prepared for the fact that you may not manage to talk about everything that is worrying you the first time you try. Starting the conversation may reveal issues you were unaware of, so be prepared to listen as well as share your worries.

- **Keep the conversation focused on your friend**, *their* feelings, *their* experience, and don't make it about you. Apart from saying that you are worried about them early on, focus on asking how they are, if anything is worrying them, if anything has changed, and let them know that your main concern is *their* wellbeing (not your own peace of mind). You might say, 'I've noticed X, and I'm worried about you ... How are you feeling?'

- **Listen to them**, don't interrupt, and *believe* what they tell you, even if you think there might be another side to the story. It's important to maintain the trust in your friendship and be supportive if you genuinely want to help your friend. Difficult conversations like these can strain relationships, but they can also form the foundations of long-term, solid, trusting friendships for life if you really care about each other and want to find a solution.

- **Don't try to fix your friend's problems**, but offer to help and support them to find solutions or change their behavior if that is what they want to do. You cannot make people change if they are not ready, only encourage them to consider how life might be better if they did make changes. They will change when they are ready and with support, if they need it. If they want to talk to a professional, you might offer to go with them to the appointment then wait in reception for them, or sit with them as they look up online resources. Encourage them to talk to their family or people they trust for additional support too.

- **You cannot fix other people**. If they seem uninterested in what you are saying, unprepared to make changes or consider the impact their behavior is having, or cannot see what the problems are, then you will need to accept that you can either support them quietly from the sidelines until they are ready to change, or you can step back from their lives, spend less time with them, and see if they come round in time. Ultimatums don't work either, and will only create more stress for all concerned.

It is not your responsibility to sort out your friend's risky behaviors or problems (or mental health issues). Many students feel a deep sense of commitment to their friends and wish to help. This is wonderful, but it is really important to realize that your most important role is as their *supporter*, to walk alongside them on their path through life, not to try to sort things out for them – they have to do that for themselves. You can be their cheerleader, but you cannot play the game for them.

If you bear all these things in mind, and give your friend time, space and a listening, trusting ear, you should hopefully be able to help them to think about what is going on for them and what they would like to do differently (if anything). You'll be able to support them as they put their plan into action, cheering them on when they most need it.

Ask for Help if ...

If despite trying the top tips listed above you are still living life on the risky side, either because you feel indestructible or because you just don't care enough about your own wellbeing, **stop** and take a moment to think about some of the potential consequences. If you are feeling very low, and this is the only way you feel *anything*, then please do talk to someone you trust – a counselor, a doctor or your tutor – and ask for support. Support teams *want* to help you.

Unplanned pregnancies, sexually transmitted infections, injuries whilst under the influence and stress resulting from (criminal) behaviors such as dealing drugs to mates, drink-driving, or inappropriate behavior towards other students are all reasons that university doctors have compassionately supported students. If you are struggling, and worried about the impact your behavior is having on your own health, wellbeing or safety, or that of others, then please reach out for help – it is *never* too late.

However bad the situation may seem, there is *always* something that can be done to support or advise you, to help you to get back to a better place, or cope with the current challenges. It may mean being referred for specialist support, being supported to deal with the criminal justice system, or having regular counseling or therapy, but university staff have usually seen it all, and are there to help. Just ask.

CHAPTER 3

ALCOHOL

A Paradox!
That well-known philosopher (!) Homer Simpson once said that alcohol was "the cause of, and the answer to, all of life's problems."[vi]

Although it may not be quite that straightforward, it's fair to say that in most societies and cultures, alcohol plays a significant role, whether you choose to drink it or not. Alcohol use, if you think about it, can feel like a paradox to get your head around. It is legal, widely advertised and marketed, talked about constantly and openly, and yet responsible for thousands of deaths every year. Other potentially dangerous substances such as smoking are similarly harmful, but promotional marketing is minimal if not actively discouraged, and, of course, recreational drugs are illegal as well as being more hidden in society. So what is the deal with alcohol?

Why Drink?
Alcohol brings both pleasure and pain. So it is not really surprising that many students use alcohol both for fun and relaxation, but also to hide their discomfort, cover up anxiety, or numb their emotions. It's a socially acceptable – and often encouraged – method of stress relief. It's legal, used frequently for "self-medication", yet highly dangerous in excess, or combined with certain activities (e.g. driving)

or drugs. Its use is widespread, yet *fewer* young people than ever before are drinking regularly.

Why Avoid Alcohol, or Reduce Your Intake?

Some of the increased risks associated with alcohol are:[vii]

- Health risks, including more mental health issues.
- Accidents and injuries.
- Unplanned pregnancy.
- Unprotected sex – sexually transmitted infections.
- Unplanned time off studies or work.
- Loss of personal possessions.
- Risk of violence or antisocial behavior.
- Financial cost.

Fewer students are drinking alcohol, but when they do they tend to 'binge drink' [viii]

More students than ever before are identifying as non-drinkers (one in five *never* drink), but when students do drink, many tend to drink most of their recommended weekly limit *in one go*, and sometimes drink more than that, leading to "binge" drinking. Only 3.7% of US students drink every day![ix]

It may therefore be easier to say, 'No, thank you,' to alcohol if you want to than you might have thought with such a high chance that others around you won't be drinking either. However, if you are going to drink, keep your consumption moderate and at least try to avoid binge drinking, which puts you at a much higher risk of accidents, falls, violent incidents, heart problems, or mental health issues.[x]

Olly's Story

Olly went to see the university doctor halfway through his first year, by which time he was already facing disciplinary proceedings for criminal damage to university property, following one of many drunken episodes. Since arriving at university he had struggled with social anxiety, getting very stressed about meeting new people, the constant pressure to impress others, and worrying about what others thought of him. To cope with those feelings and to distract himself, he drank.

First of all, he drank enough to get through the parties and social events, then a little to get through lectures, then alone in his room, getting angrier and more distressed as the hours passed. He had finally reached the point when one night in his hall he had broken a chair by throwing it down a stairwell and had inadvertently also damaged an expensive chandelier on the way down. The university had taken action, and he was now sitting in front of the doctor asking for support, and keen for intervention. His dad was with him and supportive, and his university academic department was strongly encouraging him to take positive action to stop his drinking. Fortunately, there were several helpful options available to Olly, both to reduce his drinking and his social anxiety (including talking therapy). The GP listened carefully, then outlined what the next steps might be. And as he was being so proactive in seeking help, the university dropped the charges.

Healthy Approaches to Alcohol – What You Can Do

Staying safe – how do I drink sensibly?

There are, of course, internationally recognized "safe-drinking" limits, and it is strongly recommended that to remain healthy and safe you follow these.

Recommended alcohol limit for men and women in the UK

- Fourteen units per week ideally spread over three or more days.

- Avoid binge drinking (i.e. drinking most of your intake at one time).
- Try to have alcohol-free days each week.

See the table below for definition of a UK "unit" (may vary worldwide) and how that relates to what you might be drinking. Work out what your current drinking level is every week – how many units are you having? Are you within the recommended limits?

Type of drink	Number of alcohol units
Single small shot of spirits* (25ml, ABV 40%)	1 unit
Alcopop (275ml, ABV 5%)	1.4 units
Small glass of red/white/rosé wine (125ml, ABV 12%)	1.5 units
Bottle of lager/beer/cider (330ml, ABV 5%)	1.7 units
Can of lager/beer/cider (440ml, ABV 5.5%)	2 units
Pint of lower-strength lager/beer/cider (ABV 3.6%)	2 units
Standard glass of red/white/rosé wine (175ml, ABV 12%)	2.3 units
Pint of higher-strength lager/beer/cider (ABV 5.2%)	3 units
Large glass of red/white/rosé wine (250ml, ABV 13%)	3.3 units

*Gin, rum, vodka, whiskey, tequila, sambuca. Large (35ml) single measures of spirits are 1.4 units. *Source: NHS Live Well*[xi]

Looking at the table above, if you had a couple of pints of strong cider at the pub one evening after lectures, you're nearly halfway through your weekly recommended allowance already, so it is useful to keep this in mind when going out or having a drink at home. Following government guidelines should minimize the risk of harm coming to you, either directly from drinking alcohol or from the effects of the alcohol making you less alert, less able to defend yourself, or more vulnerable.

How to consume alcohol with care

There are many ways to reduce how much you consume, which might mean you also have more fun and don't feel so awful the next day! Here are a few suggestions:

- Drink slowly (and keep a tally of your intake).
- Avoid drinking games and initiation type ceremonies.
- Eat healthy carbs (dips and bread, not fried food) before and during drinking.
- When drinking alcohol also have a non-alcoholic drink on the go. Take alternative sips from them both to space your alcohol consumption, or have a non-alcoholic drink between alcoholic drinks.
- Don't drink straight after heavy exercise; you will feel worse because your blood sugar levels drop from both the exercise and alcohol, leaving you feeling light-headed, or washed out.
- Don't mix drugs and alcohol; the combination is much more dangerous.

Alcohol-free university life

If you want to try some non-alcohol related alternatives for going out then plenty of universities now have "café crawls" instead of bar crawls, cake and coffee events or pizza and film nights in their residences. Alcohol no longer has to be the glue holding together your social activities, and plenty of students are able to avoid alcohol whilst still making friends and meeting new people.

Alcohol-free residences are also now an option in many universities, as are "quiet halls", which provide a calmer environment even if not strictly alcohol-free. If you think you might struggle to keep your drinking under control at university, it may be helpful to look for new ways to get together with others in non-alcohol-fuelled scenarios, or choose to live in an alcohol-free residence.

It feels too difficult ...

Following this advice will hopefully help you to feel more in control and comfortable with your drinking, and to be able to say no if you don't feel like drinking. However, for some people, even if they are trying their hardest, it can be almost impossible to stop drinking too much. They need more help, usually professional help such as from medical staff or specialist charities, and universities are well placed to provide this, either through their own support services, or sometimes because they host visiting groups, such as Alcoholics Anonymous, on campus. Ask a member of the wellbeing team if this is an option where you are.

Problem drinking is particularly difficult to stop in our society, where drinking is normalized and celebrated, so you will not be alone if you need more support. If you're not sure if you or your friend's drinking is a problem, this section outlines when students should consider taking additional action to review and curb their drinking, or stop (abstain) altogether.

Supporting a Friend who is Drinking Too Much

Much of the advice for supporting a friend who is taking risks in Chapter 1 will apply here too, of course, as the principles for helping someone change their behavior are the same whatever the context, but here are a few specific pieces of advice for managing alcohol as part of the situation too.

- **Don't try to discuss issues when they are drinking, or drunk.** Try to find a time when you are both feeling calm and relaxed. Before bringing up the subject of their drinking, try to be clear in your own head what your own limits and boundaries are when you think about their behavior. For example, you might tolerate being there to help them get home at the end of the night or hold their hair back when they vomit, but you should absolutely not tolerate violence or criminal activity.

- **You may like to talk to other friends first** before talking to the person you are worried about to see if they have any other information to help you consider your options.
- **Don't facilitate their drinking** by buying them alcohol or drinks, making excuses or lies for them when things go wrong, or lying to them about the impact their drinking is having on others. Let them sort out their academic problems, or relationship issues themselves. Don't offer to speak to their tutor on their behalf, but help them to book the meeting with the tutor if they need help. If they start to feel the negative impact of drinking on their own life, they are more likely to take action to address it. The drive to do anything differently might be delayed if you help them, even if you mean well.[xii]
- **Offer to go with them to seek professional help**, either to the doctor, a counselor, or an AA (Alcoholics Anonymous) meeting locally. It may take a few attempts to get them there, but don't give up on them, as long as it is not having too stressful an effect on you.
- **If you need support too, then make sure you also talk to someone helpful.**

Ask for Help If ...

You will probably need more professional and ongoing help if you have noticed yourself drinking to deal with anxiety, stress, social occasions or to get through the day. If you are drinking to help you sleep (it won't), or to cope with grief. If you are drinking alone. If you are drinking enough to upset your friends, partner, relationships or family, or if you have had it suggested to you that you should think about cutting back a bit. If drinking is costing you money you can't afford, or badly affecting your studies, or even leading you into trouble with the law, then it is time to talk to a professional (or a friend, if you need help to get to a professional) about what is happening for you, and how you are feeling.

Take action now and don't let things slide. The earlier you seek help, the better and, as with so many things in life, the sooner you can get back on track.

This book is not about scaremongering – its aim is to ensure that you make informed decisions about any risks you wish to take. And you can always ask for more specialist or medical help and advice should you need it.

CHAPTER 4

DRUGS

What do we Mean by "Drug Use"? We Mean Any Drug Use!

It is not uncommon when talking to students about drugs to hear comments such as, 'Oh, I don't really use them – just a bit of cannabis, MDMA and ketamine for fun.' The unspoken (incorrect) implication being that if you're not using "hard drugs" (such as heroin), you're "not a drug user". So it's important to be very clear about your drug use, and be honest with yourself if you are using them, for whatever reason.

If you are using drugs, including cannabis, cocaine, MDMA, ketamine or Xanax among others, then you need to think about *why* you are using them (perhaps for fun, boredom, to be part of a friendship group, or to "help" mood/sleep issues?) and try to keep your risk to a minimum. Obviously, students use drugs when partying, but they also commonly use them to "self-medicate" – to overcome shyness, insomnia, anxiety about social situations, or feeling down. The irony is that whilst the drugs may feel like they're helping in the short term, the reality is they make most mental health, anxiety or sleep problems worse in the longer term.

One of the biggest risks with drugs use is the slippery slope towards dependence. You start using something to help you relax or sleep or because you're bored, and then, before you know it, you need a bigger dose or to take it more often to get the same beneficial effect. There is a very fine line between using for fun and using because you need to. That is when drug use becomes a problem for many people.

Being honest about your use

Many young people who use drugs mistake being high for being happy. Drugs make them feel different and take them away from their worries or stress, and this in itself can feel like "happiness" and a reason to use again.

Being honest about your own situation and why you use drugs can help prevent you from going too far, or nudge you to get help if it has slid into *problematic* use. Denial that there is an issue is a key part of problematic drug use, so if you hear yourself telling anyone who's worried about you that you're fine, thank you and no, you don't need any help or intervention, then maybe it's time to reflect and think about why they are asking about your drug use.

Think about how often you use and how much you use now, and compare it with how much you needed in the past to get high or to sleep.

Amit's Story

Amit was a school sports star and arrived at university ready to participate and compete at a high level, alongside studying for his full-time course. He was fit, healthy and a high achiever. His view of drugs was of people "shooting up heroin", and so when he was offered his first smoke of weed at a university party, he wasn't too worried about saying yes; he considered his body to be at peak physical fitness and therefore able to cope with any mild "pollution". What harm could it do? And it might help him to fit in ...

He was unprepared for how euphoric and relaxed it made him feel, how the world seemed brighter and time slowed down. As the weeks and months passed, Amit found himself smoking cannabis more often, trying to regain that initial high and using it to relax with friends, or alone, to sleep and as a "treat" after working hard all day. An occasional habit slowly turned into a daily habit, and other drugs crept into his life. He started being late for sports practice, and missing lectures or seminars.

Eventually, his tutor caught up with him, and within a week of that, his coach had also reached out. People were really concerned, and Amit realized that it was time to talk to someone, to ask for professional advice and take a good hard look at his friendship group, those that used drugs and those that didn't, and make some changes in his life. Amit was fortunate to have good friends (and supportive university staff) to speak to, as well as lots of options for help in the wider world. Getting back on track took a while and was not easy, but it was absolutely worth it. The slippery slope had caught him out, and had almost led to significant academic issues, as well as having a negative impact on his personal and sporting life.

Healthy Approaches to Using Drugs

Avoiding the slippery slope (to reduce risk)

- **Take a cold hard look at your drug use.** It can help to take a moment to reflect on how much you are using, and how often at the moment. Are there only specific circumstances in which you use drugs, or is the setting and context irrelevant? Has your use increased, or the pattern of what you choose to use changed? Be honest.
- **Get some control back if you need to; stay safe and be better informed.** If you want to just use on Saturdays,

then don't start using on Wednesdays because you're bored. Watch for changes in your pattern of use. If you're using most days just to "get through the day", then please do talk to someone professional for support to help you deal with whatever is underlying your need to use.

• **Check out some credible sources of information** (not your mates or online forums), and ask for help if you need it. Reliable resources are listed at the back of this book.

Festival safety

If you're going to festivals, get your drugs tested for free to check their *purity* (how much of the substance is actually the drug you were expecting) and *profile* (what else is mixed in). Purity and profile are what essentially define the *safety* of what you take. Take the opportunity whenever it is offered to have your drugs tested. Thousands of people now do this with organizations such as The Loop at UK festivals.

Think about what your triggers or cues are

We tend to have certain situations or experiences in life that trigger us to use, such as relationship stress, social anxiety, academic pressure or difficulty sleeping. Think about how you might find other ways to tackle those stresses or challenges. Plan what to do instead of using drugs when these situations arise.

Create a team of helpers around you

Get a good friend to help you if you need more than your own willpower to get through trigger situations. Ask your family if you think they will be supportive. Doing this alone can feel impossible, so recruit people you trust and who care about you to be alongside you. As Elizabeth Burton-Phillips MBE, founder of DrugFAM, says, 'Addiction is not a spectator sport. Eventually all the friends and family get to play, and they become the forgotten victims.' Your family and friends will want you to be ok, and it will also help them to help you.

Beware of vulnerable dates

Reducing your risk by putting yourself in a safe place at times of either celebration or stress, for example, at Christmas or birthdays. The message here is to have fun but be with people you trust, especially at vulnerable times.

Try new strategies for stress management

Search out and try alternative coping strategies, depending on what is leading you to use (sleep, anxiety, boredom, friendship group). See Chapter 9 on self-care for specific ideas. Address the underlying problem, such as anxiety, to avoid needing the drugs to cope with it.

Consider a mental health assessment with your doctor

If there are underlying mental health or stress reasons behind why you are using, then take a good look at those and talk to a professional about finding better ways to address them, whether through counseling, talking therapies, or even medication, if that's what your doctor recommends after discussion with you (this will always be your decision).

Try out alternative ways to make yourself feel good if you deserve a "treat"

If you use drugs as a reward for working hard, for example, then try to find other ways to give yourself a pat on the back, that make you feel good, but won't be so risky. Some suggestions were discussed earlier (Chapter 1) for rewarding yourself in a healthy and sustainable way that will give you a thrill but be less dangerous.

Supporting a Friend who is Using Drugs

As we have mentioned in the previous chapters, supporting a friend who is using drugs means remembering that they have to *want* to take responsibility for themselves and you cannot "fix" them. "Rescuing" people or trying "interventions" is a road to disappointment. People make their own choices in life, but you can be supportive, consistent (there for them if they need you), talk about safety, and be ready to help if they want to make changes.

- **Have a *conversation* not a *confrontation*.** Don't attack them. Avoid anger and allow them to open up if they want to.
- **Try to avoid a tone that implies that you know better than they do**, or that you are judging them. Try to be compassionate and understand that they may have specific reasons for using this particular coping strategy or distraction in their life.
- **Simply trying to convince them of the dangers of drugs will probably lead them to ignore and avoid you** if they are not ready to hear about the problems. Try to care for them without intervening directly.
- **Help them to avoid places or situations that may trigger them** to want to use. Stick to non-drug user friendship groups and help them to keep busy and focused on other activities.
- **Tell them that you are available (within reason)** if they need someone to talk to because they want to use but are trying hard to distract themselves from that craving.
- **Look after yourself too and ask for help if you need it.**

Ask for Help If ...

The advice here is very similar to the advice for alcohol use as it is important to seek support and professional advice if your drug use is escalating, if you are using them in a way that impacts badly on your relationships, your finances, or your studies, or if it is making you feel worse, more anxious, more depressed, or your sleep is deteriorating.

You are not alone, but it is important to reach out as drug use is often associated with poor mental health and so the sooner you get help, the better! Getting help is a really positive step for your future and for your health.

There will be many professional support staff on campus who can help with drug issues, and some campuses have visiting charities or agencies who run clinics or groups on site to help students reduce drug use.

Local charitable organizations will be open to students who live in their area, so look beyond the campus if you would like more help, and other helpful resources are listed at the back of this book too.

You don't ever have to do this alone!

CHAPTER 5

GAMBLING (AND GAMING)

How and Why Students Gamble (and Game Online)

Students turn to gambling for different reasons, but many see gambling as a potential way to help them raise much-needed cash for living costs. Their gambling may be via traditional cards or games at casinos, betting shops, or slot machines in the arcade, or might be in-game (via loot boxes or rewards) or online. They may also be using gambling to distract themselves from (or to help cope with) day-to-day stress, or their gambling and gaming may have started out as a fun activity with friends.

Ironically, however, gambling (which often starts as an occasional distraction with the bonus of making some quick cash) can spiral into unmanageable debt, the loss of relationships and insurmountable academic problems (through wasting both money and time). Additionally, in the context of rising student costs, high rents and, for some full-time students, difficulty having a job as well as studying, it is understandable that students might look for alternative, although more risky, ways to make a living. Undoubtedly, gambling and gaming (which can incorporate gambling behaviors) have now become a part of many more students' lives.

Why gambling is particularly high risk for young adults

Your brain starts developing before you are born and continues to do so until about the age of twenty-five, with the *last* area to mature being the zone that controls impulsive behaviors and risk-taking decision-making. The teenage/ young adult brain "lights up" with excitement at risk-taking, but has yet to develop the full capability of controlling the impulse to act on it.

You can, therefore, see how you might be most likely to get a big buzz from activities that involve risk whilst being least able to stop yourself and "just say no". As a young person, the part of your brain that helps you to control impulsive behaviors may not have fully developed yet.[xiii] This puts you at greatest risk of getting caught in that spiral of gambling, losing money, trying again, losing again, occasionally having enough of a win to keep you tangled in the web, and then losing again. You can be vulnerable to your impulsivity, and poor decision-making, and sometimes struggle to delay your need for instant gratification. An occasional bet becomes a regular wager, then more and more debt is built up.

It is not an excuse, and all humans have to learn to control impulses and risk-taking, but you can see how young people may be at more of a disadvantage when faced with the excitement of gambling or gaming as they have less of an inbuilt ability to stop – and get more of a thrill from taking part.

Student finance put at risk?

Young people starting at university may be handed "free money" to use as they wish for the first time in their lives, which can make it much harder to resist gambling, especially if they have an addictive nature. This "free money" might potentially include loan funding, bank overdrafts and grants or bursaries, but in many cases it is still not enough to live on. Sometimes students gamble their newly acquired funds in an attempt to earn some more cash, but often it is just to survive.

Inevitably they will eventually lose – the house always wins. And so, they start "chasing their losses", trying to win back what they have lost, but the spiral is always downwards overall and can have a disastrous impact on their life.

Mo's Story

Mo had been at university for a couple of years when his finances started to get particularly tricky. His dad had died and there was little money available from his family, so he began to look around for some new sources of income. His course was hugely demanding, so he tried to get a low-level part-time job, but it was hard to maintain. One day a friend mentioned in passing that he had been lucky on a horse race and won a hundred pounds from a small bet. Mo was curious. Could this be the answer to his problems?

He took out the maximum overdraft he could and went online. The choices were endless. He started to gamble, winning small amounts occasionally, but losing more. It was exciting and compulsive, and he spent more and more time betting and playing games online, alone in his room. His friends missed him and commented on his absence, but Mo was determined to make enough money to survive on, to avoid asking his family for the cash he desperately needed. He believed himself to be doing something useful and practical to help himself cope with his financial stress.

His work suffered steadily, and some friends fell away. One day there was a knock on his door. It was a university wellbeing advisor, who had been alerted by Mo's academic tutor about his declining work standards and absence from the course. Mo was dismayed to realize how things had deteriorated. The advisor talked with him for a while and they agreed to meet again. In time, Mo realized just how bad things had become and how he might need professional help to get out of his current situation, and the university teams were willing and prepared to help him. He could turn things around, but he would need their support. It was the beginning of recovery, but it would take time.

Healthy Approaches to Reduce the Risk of the Downward Spiral of Gambling (or Gaming)

Assess your personal risk level

The best way to avoid the gambling/gaming spiral is to be aware of the dangers but also of your own *personal* vulnerability or risk. For example, if you have a blood relative who is struggling with addiction, then this is a warning sign for you that you may also be more at risk of developing such issues.[xiv] Problem gamblers in the family should be a red flag for you.

Don't drink and gamble

Alcohol significantly reduces your ability to control impulsive behavior so avoid making yourself more vulnerable. Remember, you are not James Bond and this is not *Casino Royale*! Only gamble what you can afford to lose and be prepared to lose overall – don't use gambling to make money.

Pick slow gambling games

Fast betting games are much worse for letting a gambling habit slide out of control, so avoid roulette and online betting options. Try to pick slower games if you can, such as poker or blackjack.

Ask someone to help you reduce your access to money

If you know that you are likely to be given (or inherit) money or to be given student finance funds to manage by yourself, it may be sensible to *delay* the process or hand over control to someone you trust until you are more confident in your ability to control your impulses. In this way, you minimize your risk of losing important funds.

Keep the negative effect on your bank balance to a minimum

Pay bills and essential debts before you gamble. Never take credit cards or cash cards out with you. Set a limit and stop there if you're going out to gamble, and (if you can) set a limit on online betting accounts too.[xv]

Alternatives to gambling/gaming

If your friends suggest poker night as a fun activity, try to steer them towards less risky pursuits, like board games, non-betting card games, karaoke, watching a sports event together or cooking dinner together. If you need a high-adrenaline activity, try go-karting or trampolining, which are fun but generally safer for your bank account! There are plenty of things you can do if you are alone, of course, but it might be harder to resist the urge to play. Think about whether it might be better to be with others at first until you feel confident you can resist the online betting websites/shops/casinos alone.

Spend time with non-gamblers or gamers

One of the best ways to protect yourself (and your bank balance) is to spend time with family and friends who don't gamble or game. They will have other interests and this will help to distract you from any drive you have to spend a lot of time and money in ways that are ultimately damaging to you and your wellbeing. Join new groups or clubs with other interests and learn some new skills.

Supporting a Friend who is Gambling or Gaming Too Much

You may be worried about someone you care for, but as with all potentially addictive behaviors, they may not have the insight to see what's happening as a problem, or have the ability to "just stop". Here are some approaches that might help you to raise their awareness of whether their gambling is heading towards the downward spiral.

- **Approaching the topic is challenging,** so compassion and understanding will be key.
- **Letting them know that you are worried about them is OK, but do it in a non-judgemental way.** Say that you're worried they may be spending too much money or time on their activity and that you just want to know if everything is okay, and if you can help in any way.
- **Mention other areas of their life that may be affected,** like their studies, or friendship groups.
- **Say that you are happy to go with them to ask for help** if they would like.
- **Understand that they may not respond well the first time you say any of this,** but if you can, try to stick with them, and go back and offer support a few more times, if you feel comfortable to do so. But remember, you are *not* responsible for their wellbeing; they are. All you can do is offer to help and be supportive.
- **Do *not* lend them money.**
- **Help them to avoid situations where they might be able to gamble** by suggesting activities which will be fun or exciting but don't involve betting. The movies, go-karting, bowling or live comedy are all options in most campus environments.
- **Share with them healthcare or other resources available** for young people struggling with similar issues. There are online, group and clinical support

services which are free to all. (See Chapter 11 for
sources of more information and support.)

Ask for Help If ...

When you take stock of your life and look at how
gambling or gaming might be affecting it, you think you
might need to reduce the time you are spending on it
(down to an hour a day, for example) or remove it from
your life completely.

You will probably need professional support if:

- You are losing money you can't afford to lose.
- You are damaging your relationships by spending
  time on gambling/gaming instead of with those you
  love, or if you are lying to them about your habits.
- Your academic work is suffering. You're staying up too
  late and not getting work done, or if you're too tired
  to study.
- You are borrowing money – or worse, stealing it –
  to keep gambling/gaming.
- And if the overall trend in all your behaviors is
  towards poorer quality of life, friendships,
  relationships, academic outcomes, and
  emotional health.

If these warning signs are apparent, don't delay, ask your
university or health support team for help.

CHAPTER 6

FOOD AND EATING ISSUES

You Can't Avoid Food in Life, but You Can Address Eating Issues

If food or eating behaviors are what you use to help you cope with stress, then it is fair to say that these can be tricky to deal with. Whilst you can probably live a life completely free of alcohol, drugs and gambling if you need to (because total abstinence is an *option*), you cannot live a life free of all food. You might decide never to enter a bar again, or never to visit a gambling website but you are unlikely to have the option never to enter a kitchen or restaurant again, so you will need to have lots of support, a pretty strong plan and some clear boundaries if you are to tackle difficult food or eating behaviors. If they are your main coping strategies when distressed, then abstinence is not an option.

Eating disorders

Many people use food to distract from stress, or control difficult emotions, or create security in their lives, others do the same with eating behaviors, and, of course, many people use food as a reward. We will address these issues in this chapter, though we will not cover specific eating disorders (such as anorexia, bulimia and binge eating disorder) in a great deal of detail, as they would require a whole book to themselves and often need the support of professionals to recover from fully in the longer term. They are, if you like, at one end of the food/eating spectrum that we will describe but cannot completely encompass in one chapter.

Instead, we will try to illustrate and describe some food and eating issues that can commonly arise for students, what to watch for and when to get more help, as well as suggesting a few helpful things you can try for yourself.

Eating patterns

When you are stressed, you may be someone who eats too much at one sitting (binges), eats too much then tries to remove/compensate for the calories (purges), or eats too little (restricts or starves themselves), perhaps to retain a feeling of control in your life.

Alternatively, you may not eat so much that you feel *overly full* but you may use food as a reward or treat for a good job done, or to cheer yourself up. If this behavior is an occasional occurrence, then whilst it may not be the healthiest approach to food, it is likely to be manageable and sustainable, and not make you unhealthy.

You may still wish to think about finding better ways to cope with life's up and downs, and this chapter may still be helpful, but realistically, *occasional* use of food as a reward may not be problematic.

It's also important to remember that having eating issues *now* doesn't necessarily mean you will have them your whole life and you *can* return to a normal pattern of behaviors, the same as other people who don't use food to cope with stress or distress.

The Slippery Slope of Food

As with other unhealthy coping strategies, there is, unfortunately, a slippery slope. One significant issue with using food as a reward or coping strategy is how easily and quickly you can slip into a vicious cycle without realizing. This can then stop you using other, better coping strategies for stress or worry.

One way to address this is to develop a range of coping techniques. (This would apply not just for those who use food, but also for alcohol, drugs and other unhealthy techniques.) In other words, don't just have one go-to reaction i.e. reaching for the cake and cookies) but have *several* things you can do to deal with a difficult or bad day or event.

Riley's Story

Riley was a first-year student who had been struggling with his sexual identity for a few years. He had hoped that things would be different at university and he would be able to tell people he was gay. Unfortunately, things had not turned out that way. Despite the years of bullying at school, he still hadn't spoken to his father about it by the end of the first term, and, as his mum had died when he was eleven, he felt quite alone.

Riley was struggling to find the words to tell people how he was feeling and would have liked support, but he didn't know where to turn. He was also finding the "little fish in a big pond'" academic challenge greater than he imagined. The workload was proving a bit much for him, and exams were looming.

With everything starting to feel out of control, Riley tried to make himself feel more secure by slowly restricting what he allowed himself to eat. First, it was less meat, then dairy, then carbs. He told himself it was "healthy eating" and felt relief at being in charge of at least one area of his life. He went home for Christmas, worked hard for his exams, and restricted his food more and more. His weight fell, but then he started to feel urges to binge eat; it was very distressing. One day, he started eating toast and found he couldn't stop. Whilst he was being sick after the toast binge, his friend James called by and was shocked to see how unwell Riley looked. Over the next few weeks, James persuaded Riley to seek help and talk to a counselor about his eating and food issues, and in time Riley was referred, via his doctor, to a specialist mental health team, for talking therapy and longer-term eating support. Riley responded well, but if he had left it for months or years before getting help, he might have found it harder to recover.

Healthy Approaches if Food and Eating – Too Much or Too Little – is Your Reward or Coping Strategy

Be proactive and decide what you might try next time you need cheering up

See a friend, watch a comedy program, paint a picture, walk the dog, but make sure that food is not part of your "disaster-day" planning. Think ahead so that when you have a bad day or are dealing with problems, food is not the solution.

Take back control over the urge to binge eat

A good strategy is to *delay* your food reward, binge or purge, which can really reduce the urge to eat or make yourself sick. Delaying tactics can include phoning or messaging a friend, painting your nails, walking round the block or watching YouTube videos.

Make yourself feel good in different ways

Make yourself feel good by getting things done, achieving things that matter to you and will give you a sense of satisfaction. Ticking some things off your (actual or mental) to-do list can give you a renewed sense of purpose, and a soothing, low-key buzz of satisfaction.

Be kind to yourself

Have a clear sense of the things that make you feel nice in life, just for the *pleasure* of them. Not jobs to tackle, or work-related tasks, but activities that are fun and relaxing, such as having a bath, playing music, writing, swimming, reading, kicking a ball about and so on. Do these when you start to feel yourself drop in mood, or feel flat or anxious, and don't forget to connect with others too.

Stay connected to your "positive" friends

Contact friends and people who make you feel good to avoid isolation, which in itself can also lead to more food – and eating-related problems. Plan to meet up, or chat online, to avoid reaching the stage of diving into the jumbo-sized crisps or loaf of bread.

Tune into your feelings

Talk to friends (or to a professional) about your emotions and how you are feeling so that you are not bottling things up like a pressure cooker. Releasing the feelings will make it less likely that you will be driven to food to deal with stress. Consider keeping a diary of emotions, jotting down what you eat and when to see if there is a link between your emotions and your eating habits.

Boost your self-esteem

Whether you tend to eat too much or restrict and deprive yourself, it can be helpful to think about ways to boost your self-esteem. One way to do this can be to develop *several* things that make you feel good about yourself, not just focusing on your weight and body shape. If your body shape and weight are what your self-esteem is pinned on, then you will have little left to fall back on to boost you if they are making you unhappy.

Whilst much of your confidence might be tied up in how you view yourself and what your weight is doing, it can be really positive to think about how great your group of friends is, how good you are at singing, how well you're doing on your course, for example, so that all your self-esteem eggs are not in one basket. Then, should one area of self-esteem be more challenging for you (such as feeling down about your body shape), you can still reflect on the others and feel more positive.

Supporting a Friend who has Food or Eating Issues

The same principles apply as with previous chapters, where supporting friends who take risks, use drugs, alcohol or gamble too much was discussed. The key point is that you cannot make people change, you can only help and offer to support them as they make changes themselves when they are ready. Nowhere is this more true than for eating issues, where it can be almost painful for family and friends to watch someone they care about refusing to eat, or eating too much.

- **Approach any conversation about your friend's food or eating habits gently and with compassion.** Say that you have noticed X (e.g. their low energy, their mood change, that they are coming out less) and that you are worried about them.
- **Try to avoid commenting on specific topics** such as weight, body image or food intake.
- **Don't bring up your concerns when they are eating.**[xvi]
- **Say that you would like to help if there is anything you can do for them.** Ask if they are worried about anything in particular.
- **Offer to go with them to talk to someone**, or encourage them to speak to family and other supporters that they trust, such as a tutor.
- **Don't give up if they push back or deny there is an issue.** Revisit the topic in a week or so, still gently but make sure they know you care whilst being worried about them.

- **Denial is often part of all these unhealthy coping behaviors**, as is secrecy, so don't be put off, or persuaded to keep things secret.
- **Talk to charity helplines for advice** or a local campus support staff member if you want to think about what to do next.

Ask for Help *Soon* If ...

If your food or eating issues are getting worse at a rapid rate, if you are starting to feel unwell and can't do your usual activities (like meet up with friends or go to lectures). If the food issues are starting to take over your life, it is time to ask for help from a professional, if you haven't already done so.

If you feel physically unwell, faint, in pain, can't sleep, feel really anxious or down, or notice other physical or mental health issues, talk to your doctor. If other people are worried about you, then ask them to help you, if you need it, to make an appointment or sit with you in the waiting room when you go for help.

You are not alone, and there are lots of people who will help you, from friends and family through to professionals at your university or in the health service.

The key is not to ignore a difficult situation and let it get worse, if you can help it.

CHAPTER 7

SELF-HARM

What do we Mean by "Self-Harm"?

Self-harm can be a coping strategy used by people of all ages, backgrounds and cultures, and in this section of the book we will specifically consider the type of self-harm that is physical, rather than "any self-destructive act".[xvii, xviii] However, even within this definition, self-harm means many things to different people. To some it describes cutting, or burning your skin, to others it may mean taking an overdose, or self-poisoning in another way.

Why self-harm at all?

It usually feels quite bleak to discuss and think about, but self-harm is often used for relief, for distraction from emotional pain, for diversion from distress and sometimes even to release a little adrenaline to help someone lift themselves from their darkness.

If you imagine your distress to be like a pot of boiling water with a lid on, then the act of self-harm is like taking that lid off the bubbling pot. It provides a release of pressure and immediate relief. It may not be an ideal coping strategy, but it does work in that it distracts you from your immediate emotional pain. However, it is not a sustainable and healthy way to continue coping with distress. There are other ways to relieve that pressure, without causing yourself physical harm.

You may have harmed yourself, or you may have thought about it when you were distressed, or you may know friends who self-harm. You may also not have realized that self-harm can include punching a wall, or banging your head on a hard surface, so you might have friends who self-harm but you were unaware of what it signified. People can self-harm when they are angry, depressed, highly stressed, or numb. They may feel desperate and distraught, or nothing at all, so they cut or hurt themselves simply to feel ... something.

What self-harm is *not*

Self-harm is *not* "attention seeking" or a "phase", although hopefully the urge and need to self-harm will lessen in time so that it is not with you forever. The urge is more likely to fade if you can ask for help with managing your feelings and find alternative ways to release the build-up of pressure and emotion.

Why it is important to address self harm

Self-harm may not feel very risky to you, and you may feel that you have it under control, but it is worth being aware that self-harm, in all its physical forms, is associated with a high risk of future (more significant) self-harm and even suicide. It can lead to worse general health later in life, can become a habit, and can cause long-term physical damage and scarring.[xix] Although most young people who self-harm do not want to die, undertaking acts of self-harm increases the risk of pre-mature death.[xx]

This is why professionals, such as doctors and therapists, are very keen to know about whether you are using such strategies to cope, and also keen to help you find safer ways to deal with difficult emotions. They are not asking to be intrusive or "nosy"; they need to know as part of their risk assessment of how you are doing and to help you recover.

They should ask about self-harm sensitively. They should listen carefully when you describe your coping strategies, and they should be non-judgemental. They should help you to consider and learn new and better ways to manage feelings and distress in the future. They should be aware that it is not about asking you to "just stop" what you are doing, but about finding alternatives. Simply stopping your stress-management strategy is not going to help to you cope better when life is hard! If the health professional you have spoken to is not compassionate and non-judgemental, then consider asking to book in with a different person, perhaps one who comes recommended by other students.

Healthy Alternatives to Physical Self-harm

Whatever the motivation behind someone's self-harm, it's hard to see alternatives that will give you the same release in a safer yet still soothing manner. Below are a few suggestions that a number of young people who self-harm have come up with in order to cope with their emotional pain in ways that are perhaps healthier and more sustainable. The key is to try to reduce the risk of both physical damage and of long-term emotional and physical risk from further self-harm or suicidal behaviors.

Making a Worry List

You could make a Worry List – a list of triggers and situations that make you feel distressed and then plan what you might do instead of self-harm; pre-empt the issues and think ahead about potential solutions. Try to distance yourself from the distress and focus on what would distract you from it. If getting an essay mark might be stressful, plan ahead to go with a friend to a coffee shop *straight after* getting the result to distract you and focus on life beyond the essay. Another example might be that someone spoke to you rudely, so write it down, then think about whether this will still matter to you next week, or next year? If not, let it go. If it will, then address it calmly; talk to a friend and ask for advice if you need to.

Be kind

Try to be kind to yourself, as young people are often very harsh or self-critical of themselves. Think about what you might say to a friend in a similar situation, and how kind you would be to them. Be kind to yourself too.

Avoid negative social media

It is a sad fact that many platforms allow people to share images and text that are distressing and involve self-harm, so a really protective and positive step to take is to avoid such content, and if you feel able to, delete the negative sources, hashtags and platforms completely. Try to follow positive and uplifting accounts wherever you can, as they can be a source of support and distraction when you most need it. Feeds or hashtags relating to nature, animals, travel, positive affirmations and wellbeing could be a good place to start. But remember to take all social media with a pinch of salt; no one is going to post their missed deadlines or their cooking fails. Remember that social media is curated and not a factual representation. Even Beyoncé has a bad hair day now and again!

Physical alternatives

Some students achieve physical sensory distraction from emotional pain, for example by stroking their skin firmly instead of cutting it, drawing on it, massaging lotion into it and even painting beautiful images such as flowers on their wrist, to replace the cuts or burns of the past.

Be active

Listen to music or take a walk outside, whatever the weather. Run, swim, cycle, or do star jumps on the spot. Vigorous activity can allow the emotional pain to subside.

Safety planning

You can replace the risky behaviors (such as swallowing too many tablets) by having an agreed safe person you trust who you can phone or text. Or use a charity helpline (see Chapter 11 for more resources) when you feel at your wits' end and in need of urgent compassion and support.

Longer term

Many students try talking therapies of different sorts (cognitive behavioral therapy or dialectical behavioral therapy are examples of these) to move forwards and address the underlying issues that have led them to self-harm in the first place. This is an excellent path to recovery and self-healing if you feel able to explore what therapy is available to you where you live or study. Talk to the university counseling service, or to your doctor for help to access these.

Clare Dickens, a UK national self-harm prevention nurse, has this advice:

'Treat life like a pizza and take it one slice at a time. If you try to eat a pizza in a rush you will get indigestion, so savor it. It's the same in life, take things one problem at a time, figure them out slowly and you will feel much better for it.'

Bex's Story

Bex's parents went through a toxic divorce when she was younger and she had been relieved to leave the family home and start university. She was academically able – a perfectionist, really – and keen to move forwards in life, leaving the difficult past behind as much as possible. She threw herself into work; she put long hours in at the library and tried incredibly hard to make her essays original and well argued. However, despite all her efforts, she was devastated to receive a 2:2 in the second term. Although her tutor encouraged her not to view it so apocalyptically, Bex went home feeling very low and descended into a spiral of negative thoughts, similar to those she had had in her teenage years, feeling worthless and "a failure". Her mind turned to her previously trusted coping technique: cutting. So she found a blade, and in despair, started to scratch words into her arm such as "pathetic" and "loser".

A few days later she felt calmer, so she decided to speak to her tutor, who had seemed kind and might be able to help her do better next time. The tutor was happy to talk but also noted the scratches peeking out from Bex's long-sleeve top. First of all, the tutor explained that university learning was significantly different, more independent and deeper than school learning. Only by stretching herself – as she had – would she make progress, but that the effort involved would not necessarily result in high marks initially. She then took a breath and asked Bex if she was okay, if she would like to talk more about other worries, or to share anything on her mind. Bex was taken aback, and tearful, but gradually they started to talk, and over the next few weeks the tutor was able to encourage Bex to speak to a wellbeing professional at the university and eventually to be referred for a special talking therapy (dialectical behavioral therapy) to help her with her long-term use of self-harm and find an alternative way to cope more healthily with distressing feelings and thoughts. Bex did well, and over the next few months was able to recover and move forwards with her life, just as she had planned to, but with a little extra help.

Supporting a Friend who Self-harms

It can be really upsetting to know your friend is harming themselves because they are in distress. You will want to help, but it is important to keep some boundaries, you can be part of their circle of support, but you are not responsible for their wellbeing.

- **You might notice that their behavior is becoming more erratic;** they are moody, or unpredictable; they are cutting themselves off from you or others and talking in a more negative way (even mentioning self-harm or suicidal thinking).

- **You can offer to help them to write a safety plan,** or be part of their safety plan (see below) but give compassionate boundaries about what they can expect from you if what they are asking might be too much of you. You won't want to let them down, so you need to be absolutely clear about what you can offer. Are you the right person to be the one they call at 3 a.m. in distress, or should that be someone who is less likely to sleep through their phone ringing?, or a professional support charity? Would your supportive role be more about checking in with them every day for coffee or lunch, or making sure they don't feel like a burden to others when they are feeling ashamed or full of disgust for themselves?

- **Look after yourself too** and don't become "distress intolerant" because you have had to cope with so many of other people's problems. If you are full to the brim of other people's worries, you can't look after yourself, so make time for that too.

- **Talk to the professionals,** or your family if you are worried and unsure what to do about a friend.

> ## Ask for Help If ...
>
> You may need to seek additional support if your self-harm is worrying you, or your family and friends. Have you noticed your self-harming escalating, using it more often in more risky ways to hurt yourself than before? If you are feeling more down emotionally, more anxious, more trapped or isolated, or like you are a burden to others. And if you are harming whilst using alcohol or drugs – which can put you more at risk, too.
>
> If you are feeling suicidal, or at rock bottom, please talk to someone, look at your safety plan for advice if you have one, or follow the advice below.

When it All Gets Too Much ...

When life feels unbearable, pointless, futile, or worthless, it is not uncommon to consider whether you really want to keep going, to stay alive or to bother with life. You might say things like, 'What's the point?', think you are a burden to others and you may feel "trapped" in your life, aimless and unmotivated to carry on. All of these thoughts can lead you to consider taking your own life, and such suicidal thoughts can be very frightening and exhausting.

It may be helpful to know that up to one in five people will have suicidal thoughts at some point in their adult lives, but for most people these are fleeting thoughts and are often just in response to overwhelming stress.[xxi] They settle and pass, and we move on with our lives.

For most people who think about suicide, the negative feelings (feeling worthless, useless, unwanted, or numb) will be temporary and the person will go on to lead a life with normal ups and downs, but they will recover from the suicidal thinking. It is important to remember that even such difficult thoughts can be tolerated and managed, then left behind, in time. The key is to talk to someone you trust.

Help for suicidal thinking

If the thoughts are more persistent, however, or plans start to form in your mind, or you prepare for taking your own life (such as by stockpiling tablets, writing a note, reading about methods online, or giving away your pet) then it is really important to seek help and talk to a professional such as a counselor, doctor or psychologist on the same day, especially if these thoughts are escalating or feel overpowering.

> **I Need Help Now!**
> Immediate help is always available if you feel like this. Dial the emergency phone number 999, speak to your doctor, or go to the local hospital emergency department. Organizations like Samaritans are also available twenty-four-seven, by phone or text.
> **(Telephone: 116 123 free call.)**

Specialists and therapists want to hear from you, that is what they are there for, and so please do let them know if you are feeling like this.

Safety plans

Something that a lot of people are now doing and finding helpful is writing themselves a "safety plan" for use when times feel dark or thoughts become very negative again.

Safety plans are a tool (a set of instructions, if you like) that you can turn to, and you might have created one when you weren't feeling too bad, preferably with the support of a professional or even a university personal tutor.

The idea is to make a list (on paper, on your phone/laptop, or on specially designed apps) of specific activities to try when you feel yourself going down into a spiral of negativity. It can include useful resources, phone numbers, and websites, as well as trusted people to contact and speak to if life feels overwhelmingly difficult at that moment. The plan should be kept somewhere you can easily find it if needed, and should start with noting the signs to look out for that you are going downhill emotionally. List some activities that always make you feel a bit better (going for a walk, listening to a particular song, or watching a comedy program) and then list the people to contact, and emergency numbers if needed.

It can help to give yourself written instructions of how to keep yourself safe ("give flatmate stockpiled medication") and also to include some positive reasons for living (your family, your pet, your love of music) and so on. You can share the plan with a trusted friend or family member if you like.

Finally, you should commit to trying to use the plan, though it is not a contract – it is just a commitment to yourself to read it and act on it when you are down.

Try this

Make your own Safety Plan now:

	Safety Plan
What makes you think about harming yourself (triggers)?	
Reasons for living	

	Safety Plan
Making things safe e.g. removal of access to means	
Activities that improve your mood	
Activities to calm yourself	
Contacts (general support)	

	Safety Plan
Contacts (suicide and self-harm prevention specific)	
Contacts (professional e.g. doctor/counseling service)	
Contacts (emergency)	
Personal commitment to implement safety plan	

When it All Gets Too Much – (Quoted with permission from 'Suicidal Thinking and Behaviour', *Depression@University* by Dr Dominique Thompson, Trigger (Newark: 2019).[xxii])

CHAPTER 8

HELPING OTHERS

In each chapter you will have read about helping a friend who is struggling. You will have noticed several themes coming up repeatedly, with variations depending on the problem you, and they, are facing.

It is absolutely right and caring to try to help others, but it is also important to protect your own wellbeing as you do so, and maintain boundaries around what behavior is acceptable and what actions you will *not* tolerate.

The main themes to bear in mind when trying to help others are:

- You cannot fix other people.
- They have to want to change their behavior and make new life choices.
- Compassion and kindness will get you further than criticism, judgement or ultimatums.
- Take time to "understand the why" – *why* people do things that may be harmful to themselves (see next section for more information).
- You can't change things for them, but you can offer to be alongside them as they make changes.
- You can support them to make positive and healthier choices and be with them as they try new things, like a new activity or therapeutic intervention to improve their situation.

- Be realistic about what you can do and how much time you can spend on their problems, and if it is affecting your life negatively, think about whether or not *you* need more specialized or personal support yourself (see Chapter 9 for more self-care advice).

Understanding Why People do Things That May Harm Them

When you realize that a person you care about is harming themselves, is taking risks with their health, is developing an addiction or behaving in a self-destructive way it can be very common to become focused on the behavior – on *what* they are doing. We see the physical harm, the starvation, the pain or negativity and want to stop it – immediately, if possible.

But whilst they might need immediate care if they are in physical danger, in most situations it is important not to get distracted by or fixated on the *what* of their actions – what they are doing to themselves, what the risks are, what the long-term damage may be – but instead focus on the *why* of the behavior.

You need to understand the *why* behind the action, the risk, the pain to be able to help them. Why does this behavior feel necessary to them, why do they want to distract themselves in this way? Why is this happening? Try to understand what the problem is to which their behavior feels like a solution.

Asking kindly and patiently about the underlying reason for their self-harm, their avoidance of food, their constant immersion in online gambling, their use of drugs, whilst not getting caught up in the dangers and fear you are feeling, will slowly allow you to have a conversation that builds the trust they need to feel to share with you their *why*.

Fear of judgement

Many young people seeing their GP or therapist for such difficult and painful behaviors, ask for help because things have become too awful to bear anymore, but they may be fearful that others might judge, criticize or dismiss them, that professionals will focus on the what was happening instead of the why it had happened.

It is important to interpret difficult and scary behaviors, to empathize and to understand people's coping strategies, even when they feel risky or unhealthy, in order to better support them when they need our help.

- When they drink too much they may be doing it for fun, but sometimes it is to numb their feelings of anxiety or depression, or just to allow them to feel something.
- When they restrict food or starve themselves it is rarely about the food but about the control they are trying to regain over their life, or to feel secure.
- When a person self-harms, it is, as we have said earlier in the book, often to distract themselves from emotional pain with physical pain.
- When a young person thinks about suicide, it can often be because they fear failure and letting people down.

Just telling them to stop won't work

Just telling them not to cut, not to drink too much, or to "eat a bit more" won't work, because none of these approaches come close to addressing the *why* of their coping strategy.

If you want your friend to change their behavior and cope with their pain and distress in a safer way, then you need to be open to talking about their pain, their fear of letting people down, their fear of failure, or their lack of purpose in life, and be ready to listen.

Then you need to help them find help, to address the reasons behind or underlying their need for drugs, alcohol, gambling and so on, otherwise they will never be able to change their behavior.

They can't stop until they have an alternative way to cope with distress. This is why staging abrupt "interventions" will not be helpful.

You need to be compassionate and listen, which as a concerned friend you are already on the road to being.

What you can say

You will need to be *very clear* about your support, and your availability to have difficult conversations. You may need to address directly their fear of letting people down, for example by saying to them, 'There is nothing you could do or say that I wouldn't want to listen to or want to know, or help you with. Whatever the issues, we can sort it out. Whether it is related to bullying, relationships, sexuality, debt, addiction or exams, whatever the problem, I want you to feel able to talk to me about it.'

Remember:

- People are often scared to bring up difficult topics, but if you approach it gently, even if they brush you off, they might come back to you at a later time.
- They will know you are a good person to talk to, and confide in, as you were kind and careful with their feelings, and showed your concern.
- Don't give up if they push you away, but don't force intervention.
- Ask professionals for support if you are unsure what to do next.
- You need to spell it out, compassionately and honestly.
- Tell them that you know there might be difficult things happening for them, but that you are ready to help where you can. When they feel ready.

You can do three things for your friend who is struggling: **You need to listen to them, believe them, and you need to give them hope.**

In other words, compassion is everything. Then ...

1. **Listen** because they need to talk, and you should not interrupt.
2. **Believe** because you may be the first to do so and they may fear being dismissed.
3. And **give hope** because even if you can't fix the problem, you can help them find someone who can (a tutor, a counselor, a psychologist, a doctor).

They need to know that they have options even in really challenging situations.

LISTEN – BELIEVE – GIVE HOPE.

You can do it.

CHAPTER 9

HOW TO LOOK AFTER YOURSELF MORE KINDLY (SELF-CARE)

The "Usual Advice" Applies – and then Try a Few New Things!

This book is specifically written to help you if you have been struggling to cope with different situations in your life and want to find better ways to look after yourself and deal with the tough stuff. So let's start by saying that while all the "usual advice" about eating well, exercising a reasonable amount, getting fresh air and spending time with friends is absolutely fair enough, the priority here is actually for you to be kind to yourself. Be compassionate. In other words:

Give yourself a break!

Life is hard enough without you coming down hard on yourself too, and if you are reading this book and have got this far, then you are doing brilliantly and should be proud of yourself. Well done!

Life is not a straight path; it will most definitely "zig-zag" and have some real ups and downs, so if you can plan ahead and be ready for when these lows inevitably happen with your newly acquired healthier coping strategies in your toolkit, then you will regain your balance (and stay balanced) and be winning! It might not make the problems or traumas less painful, but it might mean that you are kinder to yourself whilst getting through them, and using less risky or negative ways to cope with them.

Take Time for Yourself

The next time something very difficult or bad happens to you, the first thing to do is give yourself *time*. Time to react and be emotional, but also think about and decide on the next steps.

- Take a breath; don't rush into a potentially harmful behavior or a spiral of negative thoughts or activities.
- Call, message or speak to a friend or family member you trust. Connect with others.
- Walk outside, take notice of what is going on around you (the traffic, the birds, the people walking by) and distract yourself from your most negative thoughts. This is harder if it's night-time perhaps, but still possible if you feel safe. Alternatively, sit by a window and notice what's going on outside.
- Read a book or poetry that uplifts you. Failing that, funny YouTube clips are a great option if you need some light relief.
- Listen to some music, put on a film, or TV show and distract yourself and buy yourself time.
- If overexercising is not your negative coping strategy, then get active and release some endorphins ('happy hormones') – go for a bike ride, a run or even do some yoga. Even a little movement will help clear your mind.
- Plan to see friends and make a timetable of planned activities – grab a coffee or go to the pub, or even cook dinner together, whatever feels safe and healthy for you – over the next few days. Structure can help and having your week planned out can make sure that you actually see people and get the support you need. Tell them to encourage you to still come, even if you feel like bailing out at the last minute!

- Locate a pet – yours or someone else's – and have lots of hugs, cuddles and feel the love (dogs are particularly good for this, but a hamster will do!). Plus you can walk dogs, which also gets you outside and exercising.
- If you feel like you're at rock bottom, review your safety plan and act on it – call for support and activate your network of care.

CHAPTER 10

IN SUMMARY

This little book is written to help you develop healthy coping strategies for when life gets difficult; to suggest ways to manage in the face of adversity, when it can be all too easy to reach for the bottle, the weed, the cake, or the slot machine; and to distract yourself and relieve your pain. It is completely normal and human to find ways to just "get through" when life is hard, and many of these ways may be unhealthy or unhelpful, but it is also wonderfully human to help and look after each other when we need care and compassion. It is likely, therefore, that on your journey through life you will need others to support you. This is normal, and nothing to be worried or ashamed of.

Dealing with stress, distress and emotional pain is part of life and you will not be able to avoid it, unfortunately. But if you can prepare yourself for those challenging times, by having a selection of good ways to cope and overcome them, then you will be better prepared and be not just one but several steps ahead of misfortune.

- **Build your network of support wherever you go**, know who you might turn to depending on the difficult issue, and have your safety net of trusted people around you. You are not alone!
- **Be ready to ask for help** and talk to people (including

professionals). Humans need other humans; we are not designed to be alone, so there is no shame in asking for support if you need it.

- Be honest about your own situation – about your use of drugs or alcohol or food, or your gambling, gaming, or risky behaviors. Denial will get you nowhere.
- Listen to others if they are warning you about your behavior or worried about you – they may have a point! We are not usually best placed to be objective about our own behavior.
- Changing behavior is tricky – habits can be hard to break – so allow for the fact that you might "fail" a few times when trying to change things, but don't give up. Revisit your friend network, your resources, your safety plan and your professional support teams as many times as it takes for you to get back (and stay) on track.

With time, and perseverance, and (usually) with a little help from others, you can find and maintain positive, healthy ways to cope with life's emotional difficulties, and stay balanced.

You can do this!

CHAPTER 11

WHERE CAN I FIND OUT MORE AND GET SUPPORT?

Risk-Taking Behaviors

Websites

- Kooth **www.kooth.com**
- Mental Health America
  www.mhanational.org/finding-help
- Mee Too **www.meetwo.co.uk**
- I am Me **www.iammeapp.com**
- Bipolar UK **www.bipolaruk.org**
- Depression and Bipolar Support Alliance
  www.dbsalliance.org
- Mind UK
  www.mind.org.uk/information-support/a-z-mental-health/
- Shout **www.giveusashout.org**
- Citizens Advice Bureau
  www.citizensadvice.org.uk/law-and-courts/
- Law Stuff UK **lawstuff.org.uk/police-and-law/if-you-are-arrested/**
- Bipolar World (USA)
  www.bpdworld.org/helplines/usa-helplines.html

Alcohol

Websites
- NHS Live Well **www.nhs.uk/live-well/alcohol-support/**
- Drink Aware **www.drinkaware.co.uk**
- Alcoholics Anonymous Friends and Family Group **www.al-anonuk.org.uk**
- Smart Recovery **smartrecovery.org.uk**
- Drug Helpline **drughelpline.org/alcohol-hotline/**
- Alcoholics Anonymous **www.alcoholics-anonymous.org.uk/About-AA/• Newcomers/A-Message-for-Young-People**

Physical Self-harm

TEDx Talk
- "Understanding Why" by Dr Dominique Thompson

Websites
- Staying Safe for Suicidal Thoughts **www.Stayingsafe.net**
- Samaritans **www.samaritans.org** or call 116 123 free from any phone
- Connecting with People **www.connectingwithpeople.org**
- Papyrus **www.papyrus-uk.org**
- Self-injury Support **www.selfinjurysupport.org.uk**
- Self-harm UK **www.selfharm.co.uk**
- LifeSigns **www.lifesigns.org.uk**
- Harmless **www.harmless.org.uk**
- In the USA **suicidepreventionlifeline.org/talk-to-someone-now/**

Apps (all free)
- *Worrybox*
- *Self-anxiety management* (SAM)
- *distrACT* – an app for young people created by experts
- *Calm Harm* **www.calmharm.co.uk**
- *Self-heal* – may be a useful tool **www.self-healapp.co.uk**
- *Stay Alive* **www.prevent-suicide.org**
- *My Coping Plan* – for writing your own safety plan
- *Student Health App* – for all health issues, including mental health

Drug Misuse

Websites
- The Loop **wearetheloop.org**
- DrugFAM **www.drugfam.co.uk**
- The Mix www.themix.org.uk
- Recovery based services like Bristol Drugs Project, local to you – Google them
- Erowid **erowid.org**
- Addaction **www.addaction.org.uk**
- DrugsAndMe **www.drugsand.me/en/**
- Narcotics Anonymous **ukna.org (also international support)**
- In the USA **drughelpline.org/ecstasy-hotline/**

Podcasts
- *Say Why to Drugs* by Dr Suzi Grace

Food issues

Websites

- Beat charity **www.beateatingdisorders.org.uk**
- Anorexia Bulimia Care charity
  www.anorexiabulimiacare.org.uk
- Eating Disorders Review (USA)
  **eatingdisordersreview.com/eating-disorders/
  eating-disorders-associations/**
- National Eating Disorders (USA)
  www.nationaleatingdisorders.org

Apps

- *Rise Up and Recover*

Gambling (and Gaming)

Websites

- Gaming: Game Quitters **www.gamequitters.com**
- Gambling: GamAnon **www.gamanon.org.uk**
- Gambling: Gam Care **www.gamcare.org.uk**
- Gambling: YGam
  www.ygam.org/university-and-engagement/
- Gamblers Anonymous:
  www.gamblersanonymous.org.uk
- National UK Gambling Clinic
  **www.cnwl.nhs.uk/cnwl-national-problem-
  gambling-clinic/**
- Young person's gaming clinic for those aged thirteen to
  twenty-five **www.cnwl.nhs.uk/national-centre-
  for-behavioural-addictions-gaming/**
- National Council of Problem Gambling (USA)
  **www.ncpgambling.org/help-treatment/national-
  helpline-1-800-522-4700/**

Helping Others

TEDx Talk
- Chapter 8 was inspired by TEDx Newcastle College, 'Understanding Why' by Dr Dominique Thompson

Website
- Helping a friend who is struggling **www.truestudent.com/blog/supporting-a-friend-or-flatmate-at-university**

Self-Care

Websites
- Student Minds **https://www.studentminds.org.uk**
- NHS **https://www.nhs.uk/live-well/**
- 5 ways to wellbeing **https://www.mind.org.uk/workplace/mental-health-at-work/taking-care-of-yourself/five-ways-to-wellbeing/**

ACKNOWLEDGEMENTS

As a GP caring for university students for almost twenty years, I have had a front-row seat in the lives of many young adults from all over the world, supporting them through difficult times, and advising them about how best to cope with life's challenges. I have used my wide expertise and experience in writing this book, but I wanted to bring you more than just my knowledge and insight for dealing with tough, and sometimes overwhelming, behaviors. I wanted to involve other top specialists too, to make sure that you receive the most up-to-date and relevant advice.

I interviewed experts in some of the topics discussed in the preceding chapters, and their advice was then woven through the text. They are incredibly experienced, highly skilled and highly qualified professionals whose expertise is outstanding. I am very grateful to, and would like to thank each of them for freely giving their time and advice to support students everywhere.

Thank you to:

Chapter 4: Drugs

- Jo Mallinson, young persons' drug and alcohol specialist, and the creator of the *BEproject* Bristol.
- Elizabeth Burton-Phillips MBE, founder of DrugFAM and author of *Mum, Can You Lend me Twenty Quid?: What drugs did to my family*.

Chapter 5: Gambling (and Gaming)

* Professor Henrietta Bowden-Jones OBE, consultant psychiatrist and director of the UK National Problem Gambling Clinic and National Centre for Gaming Disorders and honorary professor of University College London.

Chapter 6: Food and Eating Issues

* Dr Lucy Serpell, Clinical Lead for Eating Disorders, NELFT, and associate professor, University College London.

Chapter 7: Self-harm

* Clare Dickens, senior lecturer in Nursing Studies, University of Wolverhampton and chair of Wolverhampton Suicide Prevention Stakeholder Forum.

REFERENCES

[i]**Blakemore, S.** (2012) *The Mysterious Workings of the Adolescent Brain.* [Online video] TED. Retrieved from: https://www.ted.com/talks/sarah_jayne_blakemore_the_mysterious_workings_of_the_adolescent_brain?language=en [Accessed 07/11/19].

[ii]**Office for National Statistics, UK**. (2020) *Avoidable Mortality in the UK – Children and Young People.* [Online] Office for National Statistics. Retrieved from: https://www.ons.gov.uk/peoplepopulationandcommunity/healthandsocialcare/causesofdeath/datasets/avoidablemortalityintheukchildrenandyoungpeople [Accessed 16/10/19].

[iii]**Newport Academy.** (2017) *The Truth about Teens and Risky Behaviour.* [Online] Newport Academy. Retrieved from: https://www.newportacademy.com/resources/mental-health/truth-about-teens-risky-behavior/ [Accessed 16/10/19]

[iv]**Department of Health, New South Wales.** (2014) *Youth Health Resources Kit.* [Online] NSW Health. Retrieved from: https://www.health.nsw.gov.au/kidsfamilies/youth/Documents/youth-health-resourcekit/youth-health-resource-kit-sect-3-chap-3.pdf [Accessed 16/10/19].

[v]**Walsh, T.** (2016) *Empowering Teenagers.* [Online] Newport Academy. Retrieved from: https://www.newportacademy.com/resources/empowering-teens/adventure-therapy-teen-mental-health/ [Accessed 24/10/19]

[vi]***The Simpsons*** (1997) Homer vs. the Eighteenth Amendment. [TV] Fox. 16th March.

[vii]**NHS** (2018) *Alcohol Misuse*. [Online] NHS. Retrieved from: https://www.nhs.uk/conditions/alcohol-misuse/risks/ [Accessed 28/11/19].

[viii]**National Union of Students.** (2018). *New Survey Shows Trends in Student Drinking.* [Online] NUS. Retrieved from: https://www.nus.org.uk/en/news/press-releases/new-survey-shows-trends-in-student-drinking/ [Accessed 29/11/19].

[ix]**National Institute on Alcohol Abuse and Alcoholism** (2006). *Young Adult Drinking.* [Online] National Institute on Alcohol Abuse and Alcoholism. Retrieved from: https://pubs.niaaa.nih.gov/publications/aa68/aa68.htm [Accessed 29/11/19].

[x]**NHS** (2019). *Binge Drinking* [Online] NHS. Retrieved from: https://www.nhs.uk/livewell/alcohol-support/binge-drinking-effects/ [Accessed: 06/06/2020].

[xi]**NHS** (2018). *Alcohol Units.* [Online] NHS. Retrieved from: https://www.nhs.uk/live-well/alcohol-support/calculating-alcohol-units/ [Accessed 21/04/2020].

[xii]**Alcohol.Org** (2020). *Helping a Friend who Abuses Alcohol.* Retrieved from: https://www.alcohol.org/helping-analcoholic/friend/ [Accessed 29/11/19].

[xiii]**Blakemore, S.** (2018) *Inventing Ourselves: The Secret Life of the Teenage Brain.* London: Doubleday.

[xiv]**Slutske, W., Zhu, G., Meier, M., Martin, N.** (2019). Genetic and Environmental Influences on Disordered Gambling in Men and Women. *Arch Gen Psychiatry.* [Online] 67 (6), pp. 624–630. Retrieved from: https://www.ncbi.nlm.nih.gov/pmc/articles/PMC3600804/ [Accessed 17/12/19].

[xv]**Royal College of Psychiatrists**. (2014). *Problem Gambling.* [Online] Royal College of Psychiatrists. Retrieved from: https://www.rcpsych.ac.uk/mental-health/problems-disorders/problem-gambling [Accessed 17/12/19]

[xvi]**Beat Eating Disorders**. *Worried About a Friend or Family Member.* [Online] Beat Eating Disorders. Retrieved From: https://www.beateatingdisorders.org.uk/recovery-information/worried-about-friend [Accessed 30/10/19].

[xvii]**Gholamrezaei, M., Heath, N., de Stefano, J.** (2015). Non-suicidal self-injury across cultures and ethnics and racial minorities: a review. *International Journal of Psychology.* [Online] 52 (4). Retrieved from: https://www.researchgate.net/publication/286373404_Nonsuicidal_self-injury_across_cultures_and_ethnic_and_racial_minorities_A_review [Accessed 20/12/19].

[xviii]**NHS** (2018). *Self-harm.* [Online] NHS. Retrieved from: https://www.nhs.uk/conditions/self-harm/ [Accessed 20/12/19]

[xix]**Mental Health Foundation**. *The Truth About Self-Harm*. [Online] Mental Health Foundation. Retrieved from: https://www.mentalhealth.org.uk/publications/truth-about-self-harm [Accessed 21/12/19].

[xx]**Kidger, J., Lewis, G., Heron, J., Evans, J., Gunnall, D.** (2012) Adolescent self-harm and suicidal thoughts in the ALSPAC cohort: A Self-report survey in England, [Online] *BMC Psychiatry* 12 (1) Retrieved from: https://www.researchgate.net/publication/228080346_Adolescent_self-harm_and_suicidal_thoughts_in_the_ALSPAC_cohort_A_self-report_survey_in_England [Accessed 06/06/2020].

[xxi]**De Leo, D., Cerin, E., Spathonis, K. and Burgis, S.** (2005). Lifetime risk of suicide ideation and attempts in an Australian community: Prevalence, suicidal process, and help-seeking behaviour. [Online] *Journal*

of Affective Disorders. 86 (2-3), pp. 215–24. Retrieved from: https://pdfs.semanticscholar.org/7607/ f6d9276ff71f222d87378a7bd31bae902318.pdf [Accessed 25 Oct. 2018].

[xxii]**Thompson, D.** (2019). *Depression@University*. Newark: Trigger Publishing.

ABOUT TRIGGER PUBLISHING

Trigger is a leading independent altruistic global publisher devoted to opening up conversations about mental health and wellbeing. We share uplifting and inspirational mental health stories, publish advice-driven books by highly qualified clinicians for those in recovery and produce wellbeing books that will help you to live your life with greater meaning and clarity.

Founder Adam Shaw, mental health advocate and philanthropist, established the company with leading psychologist Lauren Callaghan, whilst in recovery from serious mental health issues. Their aim was to publish books which provided advice and support to anyone suffering with mental illness by sharing uplifting and inspiring stories from real life survivors, combined with expert advice on practical recovery techniques.

Since then, Trigger has expanded to produce books on a wide range of topics surrounding mental health and wellness, as well as launching Upside Down, its children's list, which encourages open conversation around mental health from a young age.

We want to help you to not just survive but thrive ... one book at a time.

Find out more about Trigger Publishing
by visiting our website:

triggerpublishing.com

or join us on:

Twitter @TriggerPub

Facebook @TriggerPub

Instagram @TriggerPub

The mental health & wellbeing publisher

ABOUT SHAW MIND

A proportion of profits from the sale of all Trigger books go to their sister charity, Shaw Mind, also founded by Adam Shaw and Lauren Callaghan. The charity aims to ensure that everyone has access to mental health resources whenever they need them.

You can find out more about the work Shaw Mind
do by visiting their website:

shawmind.org

or joining them on

Twitter @Shaw_Mind

Facebook @shawmindUK

Instagram @Shaw_Mind

Your Local Mental Health & Wellbeing Charity